FOOD IN THE CIVIL WAR ERA: THE NORTH

A Selection of Recipes

Adapted from the Original Nineteenth-Century Texts,

Brought Up-to-Date for the Modern Cook

Books in the American Food in History Series

A Selection of Modernized Recipes from

FOOD
IN THE CIVIL WAR ERA

THE NORTH

EDITED BY HELEN ZOE VEIT

Adapted by Jennifer Billock

Michigan State University Press
EAST LANSING

♾ The paper used in this publication meets the minimum requirements
of ANSI/NISO Z39.48-1992 (R 1997) (Permanence of Paper).

Michigan State University Press
East Lansing, Michigan 48823-5245

Printed and bound in the United States of America.

21 20 19 18 17 16 15   1 2 3 4 5 6 7 8 9 10

Library of Congress Control Number: 2015933881

ISBN: 978-1-61186-156-3 (pbk.)
ISBN: 978-1-60917-442-2 (ebook: PDF)

Cover and book design by Erin Kirk New

Cover illustration is from *The Cook's Own Book: An American Family Cook Book*
(New York: James Miller, 1864), front matter, MSUSC.

Michigan State University Press is a member of the Green Press Initiative and is
committed to developing and encouraging ecologically responsible publishing practices.
For more information about the Green Press Initiative and the use of recycled paper in
book publishing, please visit www.greenpressinitiative.org.

CONTENTS

A selection of recipes, updated and tested by food editor
Jennifer Billock, from

Food in the Civil War Era: The North, edited by Helen Zoe Veit
(ISBN 978-1-61186-122-8)

✳

Introduction

Cookbooks offer a unique and valuable way to examine American life in the era of the Civil War. One of the first and most obvious things they reveal is how differently Americans ate in the mid-nineteenth century. For example, Americans who could afford to do so ate huge quantities of animal products, especially meat. Middle-class cooking usually incorporated meat into every meal, and often into every dish, making use of a variety of animal species and body parts that would dizzy a contemporary eater accustomed to the poverty of modern supermarket selections. Desserts routinely called for meat products, too. Many people also ate huge breakfasts filled not just with meats but with dishes like potatoes, vegetables, beans, and pie.

Meanwhile, many of the foods that people today consider quintessential American dishes, steeped in age-old tradition, don't appear in these cookbooks at all, or appear only in unfamiliar forms. For example, there are a few recipes for apple pie, but there are many more recipes for blancmange, a popular nineteenth-century custard. There are occasional recipes for cookies, but there are many more recipes for puddings, part of the English culinary tradition that was still thriving in the United States more than eighty years after the revolution. Likewise, foods that would become mainstays of all-American cooking in the next century, like cheese, ground beef, and chocolate, play very minor roles in these recipes. In contrast, there were whole culinary genres in the Civil War era that almost totally disappeared from mainstream American cookbooks in later years, including sweetmeats, invalid cookery, and a range of homemade common drinks.

Besides showing how differently Americans ate, these cookbooks also show how differently Americans cooked. Preserving food and preventing spoilage were urgent tasks in an era before reliable refrigeration, and cooking techniques often were one and the same as preservation methods, so that menus regularly featured an array of pickles, jams, relishes, alcohols, and syrups as well as smoked, pickled, or potted meats. People in the Civil War era also routinely produced items at home that people today think of as being only available from gro-

This is an abridged version of the introductory essay "Seeing the Civil War Era through Its Cookbooks," in *Food in the Civil War Era: The North* (East Lansing: Michigan State University Press, 2014).

cery stores. Foods made at home included bread, butter, cheese, gelatin, carbonated drinks, vinegar, yeast, shortening, bouillon cubes, and ketchup and other condiments, among many other items. Yet Americans in the 1860s—especially the middle-class northeastern Americans targeted by these cookbooks—were not completely off the industrial food grid. There was already a complex system of national food transportation in place, and this decade saw the growth of early canning and meat-processing industries as well as the expansion of commercial brand names.

The cookbooks also hint at how difficult it was to run a nineteenth-century kitchen. Just operating the oven was an enormously complicated job, and sometimes a dangerous one. Heated by coal or by wood, ovens were notoriously hard to control, and cooks would not have had thermometers to help them gauge the temperature. Cookbook authors relied heavily on their readers' experience to know how hot to get the oven and how long to leave the food inside. Of course, for people with little cooking experience to draw upon, cookbooks could offer frustratingly meager help on this point.

Another development that might surprise modern readers is that Americans in the 1860s responded with growing interest to recipes whose titles loudly declared them to be foreign. These cookbooks are filled with recipes like Chicken Pillau, Calcutta Curry, Vermicelli Soup, Charlotte Russe, and Mullagatawnee Soup, among many others. Moreover, all these cookbooks, even the humblest, demanded ingredients that would have been transported across the country and the globe—from cinnamon to tapioca to coffee. The fact that these cookbook authors didn't hesitate to call for imported ingredients, even during the Civil War, is one more sign that these were *northern* cookbooks, since virtually none of these far-flung ingredients would have been readily available in the South by the middle of the war because of the blockade. But if food in the Civil War era was not strictly local, it was much more seasonal than it is today. Seasonal availability of ingredients was a serious constraint, an issue that arises in all the cookbooks.

Many of these cookbooks focused openly on thrift. Economizing was an old theme in American cookery, but it was especially relevant to families during and after the Civil War, as economizing on food took on new urgency for many. Hundreds of thousands of northern families lost husbands, sons, or fathers, and in many cases that meant they lost the basis of their economic subsistence. As many Americans knew all too well, turning the scraps left from one dinner into a palatable meal the next day could mean the difference between living within one's budget and sliding into debt.

Cookbooks offer a tantalizing glimpse of the past, but like all historical documents they offer us *only* a glimpse. In fact, cookbooks can be an especially tricky source. For the most part we don't know the most basic information about the people who read these cookbooks; in most cases we don't even know how many people bought them. We also don't know how readers might have modified the recipes, if they tried them at all, or what they thought of any dishes that resulted. And even the contents of the cookbooks themselves can be deceptive. The recipes and cooking techniques that any single author suggested don't necessarily reflect how Americans in the Civil War era actually cooked and ate. Cookbook authors made decisions about which recipes to include and which to leave out, and they based those decisions in part on guesses about what information would be helpful to readers. The fact that someone went to the trouble of recording a recipe at all meant that the writer assumed most people didn't already know it by heart.

At the same time, cookbook authors often left out any mention of the Civil War itself, even when they were writing right in the middle of it. To some extent, this is a reminder that lives went on and that dinner still appeared on most tables most nights, no matter how much the world was changing outside. It's also a reminder that daily life on the Union home front, especially in the urban North, saw far fewer devastating changes than life in the Confederacy. Yet the five cookbooks excerpted in this volume are all still very much books of their time, and the effects of war and politics on daily life is perceptible in all of them. By reading closely we can glean hints of the turbulence churning outside the kitchen window. People who are used to thinking of cookbooks as a source for recipes, and not much else, may be surprised at how much information they can reveal about the daily lives, habits, aspirations, and cultural assumptions of people in the past.

HELEN ZOE VEIT

BREAKFAST

✳ Hashed Beef

PREP TIME: *5 minutes; Cook time: 20 minutes;*
Total time: 25 minutes

SERVES 4

INGREDIENTS

2 tablespoons unsalted butter

1 tablespoon flour

1 large onion, minced

1 cup beef stock

1 teaspoon salt

2 tablespoons chopped peperoncinis

1 pound roast beef, sliced

2 slices of bread

STEPS

Over medium-high heat, brown the butter, flour, and onion. Slowly stir in the beef stock and salt. Increase the heat to medium and stir constantly until the sauce is thick, about 5 minutes.

Add the peperoncinis and beef. Heat through and pour into a serving dish.

Serve with toasted bread cut into triangles.

✳ Stewed Trout

PREP TIME: *10 minutes;* Cook time: *55 minutes;*
Total time: 1 hour, 5 minutes

SERVES 4

INGREDIENTS

2 trout fillets, skinned

2 tablespoons unsalted butter

1 tablespoon flour

1½ teaspoon ground nutmeg

1 teaspoon ground mace

½ teaspoon cayenne

1 teaspoon salt

2 cups veal gravy, or 1 cup turkey gravy mixed
    with 1 cup beef gravy

Half a lemon, thinly sliced

2 cups white wine

STEPS

Wash the trout and dry it completely. Set aside.

Over medium heat, melt the butter in a stewpan,
dredging in the flour throughout. Mix in the nutmeg,
mace, cayenne, and salt.

Add the trout and cook until slightly browned, about 3
minutes.

Pour in the gravy and add the lemon. Bring to a boil.
Decrease heat to low and cover the pan. Simmer for 40
minutes.

Uncover the pan, remove the fish, and stir in the wine.
Increase heat to medium and bring the gravy to a boil.
Boil for 5 minutes.

Pour a third of the gravy over the fish and the remainder into a sauce tureen. Serve immediately.

Baked Potatoes

PREP TIME: *10 minutes; Cook time: 1 hour;*
Total time: 1 hour, 10 minutes

SERVES 4

INGREDIENTS

4 medium potatoes, unpeeled

4 tablespoons salted butter (optional)

4 tablespoons sour cream (optional)

4 tablespoons shredded cheddar cheese (optional)

4 tablespoons chopped chives (optional)

STEPS

Preheat the oven to 375°F.

Scrub and dry the potatoes. Poke 10 to 12 holes in each potato with a fork. Bake directly on the oven rack for an hour.

Remove potatoes from the oven and cut open lengthwise. Serve with butter, sour cream, cheese, and chives.

Slapjacks

PREP TIME: *5 minutes; Cook time: 10 minutes;*
Total time: 15 minutes

SERVES 4

INGREDIENTS

2 cups milk

3 eggs

1 teaspoon baking soda

1 teaspoon salt

2 cups flour

3 tablespoons unsalted butter

3 tablespoons powdered sugar (optional)

1 tablespoon nutmeg (optional)

STEPS

Mix together the milk, eggs, baking soda, salt, and flour until smooth.

Melt the butter in a skillet over medium heat. Fry 1 cup of batter at a time, 2 minutes per side, or until lightly browned. The slapjacks should be about the size of a dinner plate.

Serve hot with powdered sugar and nutmeg sprinkled on top. Slapjacks will be thicker and more custard-like than typical pancakes.

✳ Hasty Pudding

PREP TIME: *5 minutes; Cook time: 15 minutes;*
Total time: 20 minutes

SERVES 4

INGREDIENTS

4 cups plus 1 cup water

1½ cups cornmeal

2 teaspoons salt

STEPS

Over medium heat, bring 4 cups of water to a boil.

Meanwhile, stir together the cornmeal, salt, and remaining water. Add mixture to the boiling water and stir constantly until it is thick and heated through, about 15 minutes. Serve immediately.

✳ Tea/Coffee

"OLD DOMINION" COFFEE POT.

COFFEE.

A brand name coffee pot, a luxury few Americans would have possessed in the 1860s, is described in *The American Practical Cookery Book* (Philadelphia, John E. Potter & Co., 1859):

"Boiled coffee, it is well known, is superior to coffee made after the French fashion, by straining; but, when boiled in an ordinary coffee pot, the fine aroma goes off with the vapor, leaving the infusion flat or bitter, hence a resort by many housekeepers to the French biggin. Recently, there has been patented a new coffee pot, which entirely removes the common objection of waste of strength, and flavor, by evaporation in boiling. It is called the "Old Dominion" Coffee Pot, and is made with a condenser at the top in which two bent tubes are arranged, one of which acts as a syphon. . . . As the coffee continues to boil, the vapor, loaded with the aroma, continues to pass through the tube into the water held in the condenser . . . Thus the coffee is boiled, and yet does not lose a particle of its fine aroma or strength."

PICNIC/LUNCH

✳ Cucumbers and Radishes with Butter

PREP TIME: *5 minutes; Total time: 5 minutes*

SERVES 4

INGREDIENTS

2 medium cucumbers

8 small radishes

2 tablespoons salted butter, at room temperature

STEPS

Thinly slice the cucumbers and radishes. Serve with butter for spreading.

 # Cold Ham Cake

PREP TIME: *10 minutes; Cook time: 35 minutes; Cooling time: 1 hour; Total time: 1 hour, 45 minutes*

SERVES 4

INGREDIENTS

2½ pounds cooked ham, chunked

1 teaspoon black pepper

½ teaspoon cinnamon

⅛ teaspoon ground cloves

½ teaspoon ground ginger

2 tablespoons unsalted butter, melted (optional)

STEPS

Preheat the oven to 375°F.

Finely mince the ham chunks. Thoroughly mix in the pepper, cinnamon, clove, and ginger. Add butter to moisten if the mixture does not stick together.

Firmly pack the ham mixture into an 8x8-inch glass dish. Bake on the middle rack for 35 minutes. Remove from the oven and carefully pour off the grease.

Chill in the refrigerator until completely cool. Serve in slices.

✳ Minced Salt Fish

PREP TIME: *2 hours, 25 minutes; Cook time: 25 minutes; Chilling time: 30 minutes; Total time: 3 hours, 20 minutes*

SERVES 4

INGREDIENTS

1 pound potatoes, peeled and chunked

1 pound cod fillet

6 slices salt pork

½ cup milk

1 tablespoon unsalted butter

STEPS

Boil the potatoes over medium heat for 20 minutes. Remove from the water and refrigerate for at least two hours.

Boil the fish over high heat for 5 to 7 minutes, until cooked through. Remove from the water and set aside to cool.

Once cooled, mince the potatoes and fish and mix them together. Press the mixture into a small skillet. Turn the molded fish out onto a plate and refrigerate it until it is chilled through.

Wash the skillet and fry the salt pork over medium-low heat to extract the most grease. Remove the pork, leaving the grease in the pan. Increase the heat to medium.

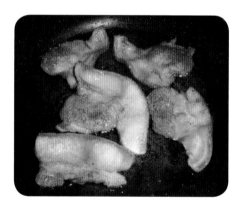

Return the shaped, chilled fish mixture to the skillet. Do not press it down. Cover and cook for 5 minutes.

Uncover and pour the milk into the center of the fish. Cover the pan again and cook for 5 more minutes.

Uncover and stir just the center of the fish mixture. Do not disturb the bottom or sides, or else a crust will not form. Cover the pan again and cook for 5 more minutes, or until heated through.

Uncover and stir the butter into the center of the fish mixture. Loosen the crust from the sides of the skillet with a knife and turn the fish out onto a dish. If done correctly, it will come out whole and browned. Serve with tartar sauce or mayonnaise.

✳ Pickled Eggs

PREP TIME: *12 minutes; Cook time: 20 minutes; Total time: 32 minutes*

MAKES 1 (1-QUART) JAR

INGREDIENTS

12 eggs

2 cups ice water

2 teaspoons salt

½ teaspoon black peppercorns

6 whole cloves

½ teaspoon ground nutmeg

2 small beets, peeled and chunked

1 cup distilled white vinegar, divided

STEPS

Boil the eggs for 12 minutes, then immediately place them into ice water to make peeling easier.

Peel the eggs and place them in a quart mason jar with the salt, peppercorns, cloves, and nutmeg. Set aside.

Boil the beets over medium heat until fork-tender, about 15 minutes. Remove them from the water and mash them. Mix ½ cup vinegar into the beets. Pour the mixture over the eggs and add the remaining vinegar.

Cap the jar and process in boiling water.

For canning: Sterilize a Ball mason jar or similar by boiling it in water for 10 minutes. Fill the sterilized jar with the prepared recipe, leaving ¼" headroom. Wipe any drips, close the jar, and set it upside down. The jar is sealed when it has made a popping sound. Once cool, label the jar and store it in a cool, dark, dry place.

Preserved Tomatoes

PREP TIME: *5 minutes; Cook time: 3 hours;*
Total time: 3 hours, 5 minutes

MAKES 1 (1-QUART) JAR

INGREDIENTS

2 pounds Roma tomatoes

2 pounds sugar

1½ lemon

¼ pound ginger root

STEPS

Blanch the tomatoes for one minute in just enough boiling water to cover them. Immediately place the tomatoes in ice water to cool.

Reduce the water to a simmer over medium heat and add the sugar. Tie the lemon and ginger in a cheesecloth bag and add to the simmering water. Use a paring knife to remove the tomato skins and add the tomatoes to the simmering water. Simmer uncovered for 3 hours.

Remove the tomatoes from the water and place them in a quart mason jar. Discard the cheesecloth bag. Pour enough of the water mixture over the tomatoes to fill the jar.

Cap the jar and process in boiling water, or store in the freezer.

✳ Mrs. Reed's Brown Bread

PREP TIME: *10 minutes; Cook time: 4 hours;*
Total time: 4 hours, 10 minutes

MAKES 2 LOAVES

INGREDIENTS

1 cup molasses

3 cups buttermilk

2 cups cornmeal

3 cups flour

1½ teaspoons baking soda

1 teaspoon salt

STEPS

Whisk together the molasses and buttermilk. In a separate bowl, mix together the dry ingredients. Stir the dry mixture into the molasses mixture until they are fully incorporated. The batter will appear grainy and have a cake-batter texture.

Fill a greased loaf pan halfway with batter. Cover the pan with aluminum foil and set aside.

Fill the bottom of a large pot with 2 inches of water. Put a steaming rack into the pot. Be sure the water does not reach the rack. Place the bread pan on top of the rack. Cover the pot and cook on the stovetop on medium heat for 4 hours, checking periodically to add more water if needed.

Preheat the oven to 425°F.

Remove the bread pan from pot. Discard the foil. Bake the bread for 10 minutes, or until browned. Remove it from the pan and place on a cooling rack immediately.

✳ Potato Rolls

PREP TIME: *2 hours, 40 minutes; Cook time: 30 minutes; Total time: 3 hours, 10 minutes*

SERVES 4

INGREDIENTS

3 large potatoes, peeled and chunked

½ tablespoon unsalted butter, room temperature

½ teaspoon salt

2 egg yolks, beaten

1½ cups milk

1 packet yeast

4 cups flour, divided

STEPS

Preheat the oven to 375°F.

Boil the potatoes over medium heat for 20 minutes, or until soft. Remove them from the water and mash them.

Place the mashed potatoes in a stand mixer with a dough hook and stir in the butter, salt, yolks, milk, and yeast. Add the flour 1 cup at a time, thoroughly mixing each time, until the dough becomes stiff.

Place the dough in a greased bowl, cover it with a damp towel, and set it in a warm place to rise for 1 hour, or until doubled. Once risen, flour hands and roll the dough into 2-inch balls. Place the dough on a tray and let it rise for another hour, or until doubled.

Bake the rolls for 30 minutes, or until browned.

Strawberry Preserves

PREP TIME: *8 hours; Cook time: 40 minutes;*
Total time: 8 hours, 40 minutes

MAKES 1 (1-PINT) JAR

INGREDIENTS

2 cups chopped strawberries
2 cups sugar, divided

STEPS

Mix the berries and 1 cup sugar together until the berries are well coated. Put in a bowl and refrigerate overnight.

The next day, over medium-high heat, boil the remaining sugar and the juice from the bowl. Add the berries. Return to a boil and decrease the heat to medium. Boil until the liquid cooks down, about 30 minutes, stirring occasionally.

Pour the berries into a jar and process in boiling water, or refrigerate for future use.

Sponge Gingerbread

PREP TIME: *15 minutes; Cook time: 12 minutes;*
Total time: 27 minutes

MAKES 2 (8X8-INCH) CAKES

INGREDIENTS

2 cups New Orleans molasses or light cane syrup

2 tablespoons unsalted butter, melted

2 tablespoons ground ginger

6 cups flour

1 tablespoon baking soda

⅓ cup water

1 cup buttermilk

STEPS

Preheat the oven to 400°F.

In a stand mixer with the dough hook, mix all the ingredients together until incorporated.

Flour a rolling pin and countertop and roll the dough out to a half-inch thickness.

Place the dough in a greased pan and bake for 10 to 12 minutes, until spongy.

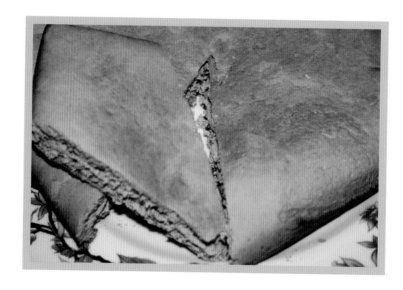

✳ Pea Soup

PREP TIME: *8 hours; Cook time: 1 hour, 40 minutes; Total time: 9 hours, 40 minutes*

SERVES 8

INGREDIENTS

4 cups split peas

12 cups plus 3 cups water

1 teaspoon salt

2 teaspoons thyme

2 teaspoons marjoram

¼ cup mushroom catsup (*recipe follows*)

1 cup cooked ham, chunked

Croutons

STEPS

Soak the split peas overnight if necessary.

Bring 12 cups water to a boil over medium-high heat. Add the peas and boil until they dissolve, about 1 hour.

Run the peas through a food mill and return to the pot. Add the salt, thyme, marjoram, mushroom catsup, ham, and 3 cups water. Return to a simmer over low heat and cook for an additional 25 minutes. Serve with croutons.

✳ Mushroom Catsup

PREP TIME: *8 hours, 20 minutes; Cook time: 2 hours, 15 minutes; Total time: 10 hours, 35 minutes*

MAKES 1 (8-OUNCE) BOTTLE

INGREDIENTS

4 cups sliced mushrooms

3 teaspoons salt, divided

1 tablespoon distilled white vinegar

½ teaspoon black pepper

¼ teaspoon ground cloves

STEPS

Put a layer of mushrooms in a deep dish. Sprinkle with 1 teaspoon salt. Add another layer of mushrooms and another teaspoon of salt. Continue this way until all have been used. Refrigerate overnight.

The next day, mash the mushrooms and juice together until they are broken down into small pieces. Mix in the vinegar, pepper, and clove. Pour the mixture into a quart mason jar and put the jar in a boiling water bath for 2 hours.

Remove the mushrooms with a slotted spoon. Do not squeeze them. Discard the mushrooms.

Boil the jar for 15 more minutes. Remove the jar from the water bath and strain the juice into a bottle. Cap and store in the refrigerator.

✳ Chicken Pie

PREP TIME: *20 minutes; Cook time: 40 minutes; Cooling time: 10 minutes; Total time: 1 hour, 10 minutes*

SERVES 8

INGREDIENTS

4 medium boneless, skinless chicken breasts
½ cup unsalted butter
½ cup flour
1 cup chicken stock
3 cups heavy cream
1 cup chopped parsley
1 teaspoon sage
¼ teaspoon rosemary
1 teaspoon thyme
1 teaspoon salt
1 teaspoon black pepper
Prepared dough for single-crust pie, or 1 box
    premade pie crust

STEPS

Preheat the oven to 375°F.

Boil the chicken breasts and cut them into half-inch chunks. Put the chicken in a 9x13–inch baking pan and spread it out to cover the bottom of the pan.

Use the butter and flour to make a roux over medium-high heat. Add the chicken stock and heavy cream to the roux. Bring to a rolling boil, whisking often so the bottom doesn't burn. When the sauce coats the back of a spoon, remove it from heat and stir in the parsley, sage, rosemary, thyme, salt, and pepper. Pour the sauce over the chicken.

For the roux: Over medium-high heat, stir together equal parts fat and flour until mixed into a thick paste and bubbling. Pour into sauce to be thickened, stirring constantly, until it reaches the desired consistency. Add more roux if necessary.

Lay the pie crust over the top of the pan. Poke two small holes in the dough. Bake for 25 minutes, or until the crust is golden brown. Let cool for 10 minutes before serving.

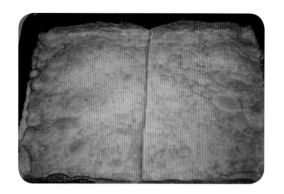

 Beef Smothered in Onions

PREP TIME: *10 minutes; Cook time: 50 minutes;*
Total time: 1 hour

SERVES 8

INGREDIENTS

6 slices salt pork

2 pounds roast beef, thinly sliced

2 medium onions, sliced

1 teaspoon salt

1 teaspoon pepper

2 tablespoons unsalted butter

2 tablespoons flour

STEPS

Fry the salt pork over medium-low heat until crisp. Set aside.

Put a layer of beef on the bottom of a stewpan. Crumble half the salt pork over the beef. Add a layer of onions on top of the salt pork, then add another layer of beef. Crumble the remaining salt pork over the beef. Add another layer of onions and continue in this fashion until all the onions and beef are used. Sprinkle salt and pepper over the meat. Pour in enough water to cover and bring it to a boil.

Decrease the heat to low, cover the pan, and simmer for 20 minutes, or until meat is tender.

Meanwhile, use the butter and flour to make a roux.

Remove the cooked beef and onions from the pan and place in a serving dish.

Bring the sauce to a boil and add the roux. Stir constantly over high heat until the sauce is thick enough to coat the back of a spoon. Pour the sauce over the beef and onions and serve.

✳ Fried Tomatoes

PREP TIME: *10 minutes; Cook time: 10 minutes;*
Total time: 20 minutes

SERVES 8

INGREDIENTS

1 cup flour

1 teaspoon salt

1 teaspoon pepper

4 large tomatoes

4 eggs, beaten

4 cups crushed saltine crackers

½ cup unsalted butter

STEPS

Mix the flour, salt, and pepper together. Set aside.

Slice the tomatoes to a half-inch thickness. Discard the ends. Dip the slices in egg to coat, then the flour mixture to coat. Dip the slices in egg again, then in the crackers to coat.

Melt the butter in a skillet over medium-high heat. Fry the tomatoes for 3 to 5 minutes per side, until golden brown. Serve immediately.

Boiled Onions

PREP TIME: *10 minutes; Cook time: 20 minutes;*
Total time: 30 minutes

SERVES 8

INGREDIENTS

2½ cups milk

2½ cups water

8 small white onions, or 2 cups pearl onions, peeled

4 tablespoons salted butter

STEPS

Mix the milk and water together in a pot and bring it to a boil over medium-low heat.

Place the onions in the pot. Boil them for 20 minutes, or until they are fork-tender.

Remove onions from the liquid and serve with butter for spreading.

Green Corn Cakes

PREP TIME: *10 minutes; Cook time: 10 minutes;*
Total time: 20 minutes

SERVES 8

INGREDIENTS

4 cups sweet corn, uncooked

6 tablespoons milk

1 cup flour

6 tablespoons plus 2 tablespoons unsalted butter

2 teaspoons salt

1 teaspoon pepper

2 eggs

STEPS

Mix together the corn, milk, flour, 2 tablespoons melted butter, salt, pepper, and eggs.

Melt the remainder of the butter in a frying pan over medium-high heat.

Drop the batter by large spoonfuls into the pan. Fry until brown, about 5 minutes per side.

DESSERT

✳ Coffee Custard

Prep time: *15 minutes; Cook time: 15 minutes;*
Total time: 30 minutes

Serves 8

Ingredients

4 cups milk

8 egg yolks

1 cup sugar

4 tablespoons brewed black coffee

Steps

In a heavy saucepan, heat the milk over medium heat until the edges froth.

Meanwhile, whisk the egg yolks until frothy. Add the sugar and coffee and stir until well combined.

When the milk is ready, slowly stir one cup into the egg mixture. Return the entire egg mixture to the saucepan. Decrease the heat to low and cook for 15 minutes, stirring constantly, until the custard coats the back of a spoon. Remove from heat. Serve hot or chilled.

✳ Bird's-Nest Pudding

PREP TIME: *40 minutes; Cook time: 1 hour, 10 minutes;*
Cooling time: 10 minutes; Total time: 2 hours

SERVES 8

INGREDIENTS

Prepared dough for single-crust pie,
   or 1 box premade pie crust
2 large apples
1 tablespoon flour
1 tablespoon water
1 tablespoon Zante currants
¼ cup loosely packed lemon peel
2 cups unsalted butter, room temperature
2 cups sugar
8 eggs, whites and yolks beaten separately
1½ teaspoons nutmeg

STEPS

Preheat the oven to 350°F.

Butter an 8x8–inch pan and line with the pastry, leaving a scalloped edge.

Peel and halve the apples. Scoop out the core to form a hollow bowl in the center of each apple.

Mix the flour and water to form a thick paste. Spread it on top of the apples' hollow side. Place the apples, hollow side up, in the pan. Sprinkle the currants onto the apples. Lay the lemon peel around the apples in the pan. Set aside.

In a separate bowl, cream together the butter and sugar. Mix in the eggs and nutmeg. Transfer the mixture to a saucepan and cook over medium-high heat for 5 minutes, stirring constantly, or until very hot. Remove from heat and continue stirring for another 5 minutes, or until lukewarm. Pour sauce over the apples.

Bake for 60 minutes, or until firm and golden brown. Let the pudding sit for 10 minutes before serving.

✳ Fruit, Nuts

Depictions of an apple (both whole and halved) and a cherry;
of grapes; and of a strawberry from *The American Practical Cookery Book*
(Philadelphia, John E. Potter & Co., 1859).

More Civil War–era recipes—as well as descriptive essays that
provide a unique portrait of Southern life via the flavors, textures, and
techniques that grew out of a time of crisis—can be found in:

Food in the Civil War Era: The South
Edited by Helen Zoe Veit
Cloth, 273 pages
ISBN 978-1-61186-164-8

AND

A Selection of Modernized Recipes from
Food in the Civil War Era: The South
Edited by Helen Zoe Veit
Adapted by Jennifer Billock
Paper, 48 pages
ISBN 978-1-61186-167-9